C000052797

Knowledge Quiz: GCSE

English Literature

Macbeth

Jennifer Webb

First published 2020

by John Catt Educational Ltd,
15 Riduna Park, Station Road,
Melton, Woodbridge IP12 1QT

Tel: +44 (0) 1394 389850
Email: enquiries@johncatt.com
Website: www.johncatt.com

© 2020 Jennifer Webb

All rights reserved.

No part of this publication may be reproduced, stored in a retrieval system, transmitted in any form or by any means, electronic, mechanical, photocopying, recording, or otherwise, without the prior permission of the publishers.

Opinions expressed in this publication are those of the contributors and are not necessarily those of the publishers or the editors. We cannot accept responsibility for any errors or omissions.

ISBN: 978 1 912906 94 9

Set and designed by John Catt Educational Ltd

How to use this book

1	Start with Quiz 1. Use the answer key to memorise the knowledge.
2	If you see anything unfamiliar, make sure you look it up or ask your teacher about it.
3	When you're ready, complete the first quiz from memory.
4	Mark it using the answer key.
5	Record your score in the quiz tracker.
6	Leave it a few days, then try the same quiz again. We've rearranged the order of the questions on the quiz sheets to further challenge your knowledge retrieval.
7	Keep completing the same quiz every few days until you get full marks every time.
8	Move on to the next quiz and repeat steps 1–8.
9	Revisit previously mastered quizzes after a few weeks or months to check you still know the content.

Important!

These quizzes will help you to master lots of the key content you need to know in order to answer questions on *Macbeth*. You must remember, though, that this alone is not enough to do well in your English Literature exam. As well as knowing all the information about plot, characters, context, terminology and quotations, you must also be able to write fluent, well-structured essays and give interpretations of the text. This book is a good starting point, but the information can only ever act as the skeleton of your writing – you need to work hard to flesh out your essays.

Below is a model response to a question about *Macbeth*. All the statements that require knowledge of facts, ideas, quotations and terminology are highlighted. This knowledge is what you will get from this book. The rest of the response comes from developing your skill as a writer.

Model paragraph

Following Duncan's murder, Shakespeare highlights the profound and terrible reality of the death of a king. Macbeth describes Duncan's wounds bleeding like a 'fountain', implying that there is a huge amount of blood and that this is a very gory and violent scene. More significantly, if Duncan is a 'fountain' and a 'spring', it suggests that, from him, all things flow like a river. This evokes the powerful and life-giving force that water has; Duncan is a divine monarch and therefore has a power that is now 'stopp'd'. This water image is also significant because it suggests that Duncan is the source of royal blood and that this has now ended. The 17th-century obsession with succession, following the childless death of Elizabeth I and the accession of a Scottish king, meant that royal blood lines were particularly prevalent in people's minds. By describing the 'stopp[ing]' of Duncan's blood, Shakespeare hints at the danger of civil war that such uncertainty creates; war was a very real fear in the minds of the Jacobean audience.

Contents

Quiz	Started?	Achieved 100%?	Revisited?
Plot and character			
1. Act 1			
2. Act 2			
3. Act 3			
4. Act 4			
5. Act 5			
Context			
6. Play origin, performance and reception history			
7. Social history			
8. Influences – the witches			
9. Influences – blood			
10. Influences – Garden of Eden			
Key term definitions and spellings			
11. Key term definitions 1			
12. Key term spellings 1			
13. Key term definitions 2			
14. Key term spellings 2			
Quotations			
15. Quotation bank 1			
16. Quotation bank 2			
17. Quotation bank 3			

Plot and character

ANSWER KEY

1.1	What happens in the opening scene of *Macbeth*?	Three witches plan to meet with Macbeth once the battle is over
1.2	Who is at war with King Duncan when the play starts?	King Sweno of Norway
1.3	Who does Macbeth split open 'from the nave to the chops'?	The traitor Macdonwald, Thane of Cawdor
1.4	What are the three predictions made by the witches in Act 1, Scene 3?	1. Macbeth will be Thane of Cawdor 2. Macbeth will be king 3. Banquo's sons will be kings
1.5	Who is made heir to Duncan's throne in Act 1, Scene 4? What title does this character have?	Duncan's son, Malcolm, Prince of Cumberland
1.6	Duncan's sons are called Malcolm and _ _ _ _ _ _ _ _ _	Donalbain
1.7	How does Lady Macbeth find out about the prophecy?	Macbeth sends her a letter
1.8	What does Lady Macbeth mean when she says Macbeth is 'too full o' the milk of human kindness'?	She thinks he is too weak to follow through with his ambitions
1.9	What do Macbeth and Lady Macbeth decide to do in Act 1, Scene 5?	They decide to kill Duncan so that Macbeth can become king
1.10	What does Macbeth mean when he says of Duncan that 'his virtues will plead like angels'?	Duncan is such a good man that, when Macbeth tries to kill him, all his good parts will beg like angels to be saved
1.11	What does Macbeth feel about the plot to kill Duncan at the start of Act 1, Scene 7?	Macbeth decides that it would be wicked to kill the king, because he is a good man, a family member, and a guest in his home
1.12	What does Lady Macbeth mean when she says 'screw your courage to the sticking place and we'll not fail'?	She means that if Macbeth is brave, their plan to kill Duncan and seize the throne will work

TRACKER

Quiz	Date	Score
1		
2		
3		
4		
5		
6		

Got it? ☐

Quiz 1: Act 1

1.1	What happens in the opening scene of *Macbeth*?	
1.2	Who is at war with King Duncan when the play starts?	
1.3	Who does Macbeth split open 'from the nave to the chops'?	
1.4	What are the three predictions made by the witches in Act 1, Scene 3?	
1.5	Who is made heir to Duncan's throne in Act 1, Scene 4? What title does this character have?	
1.6	Duncan's sons are called Malcolm and _ _ _ _ _ _ _ _	
1.7	How does Lady Macbeth find out about the prophecy?	
1.8	What does Lady Macbeth mean when she says Macbeth is 'too full o' the milk of human kindness'?	
1.9	What do Macbeth and Lady Macbeth decide to do in Act 1, Scene 5?	
1.10	What does Macbeth mean when he says of Duncan that 'his virtues will plead like angels'?	
1.11	What does Macbeth feel about the plot to kill Duncan at the start of Act 1, Scene 7?	
1.12	What does Lady Macbeth mean when she says 'screw your courage to the sticking place and we'll not fail'?	

Who does Macbeth split open 'from the nave to the chops'?	
Duncan's sons are called Malcolm and _ _ _ _ _ _ _ _	
What do Macbeth and Lady Macbeth decide to do in Act 1, Scene 5?	
What does Lady Macbeth mean when she says 'screw your courage to the sticking place and we'll not fail'?	
Who is at war with King Duncan when the play starts?	
What are the three predictions made by the witches in Act 1, Scene 3?	
What does Lady Macbeth mean when she says Macbeth is 'too full o' the milk of human kindness'?	
What does Macbeth mean when he says of Duncan that 'his virtues will plead like angels'?	
What happens in the opening scene of *Macbeth*?	
Who is made heir to Duncan's throne in Act 1, Scene 4? What title does this character have?	
How does Lady Macbeth find out about the prophecy?	
What does Macbeth feel about the plot to kill Duncan at the start of Act 1, Scene 7?	

What does Macbeth mean when he says of Duncan that 'his virtues will plead like angels'?	
What happens in the opening scene of *Macbeth*?	
Who is made heir to Duncan's throne in Act 1, Scene 4? What title does this character have?	
Duncan's sons are called Malcolm and _ _ _ _ _ _ _ _ _	
Who is at war with King Duncan when the play starts?	
What do Macbeth and Lady Macbeth decide to do in Act 1, Scene 5?	
How does Lady Macbeth find out about the prophecy?	
What does Macbeth feel about the plot to kill Duncan at the start of Act 1, Scene 7?	
What does Lady Macbeth mean when she says Macbeth is 'too full o' the milk of human kindness'?	
What does Lady Macbeth mean when she says 'screw your courage to the sticking place and we'll not fail'?	
Who does Macbeth split open 'from the nave to the chops'?	
What are the three predictions made by the witches in Act 1, Scene 3?	

Duncan's sons are called Malcolm and _ _ _ _ _ _ _ _	
What does Lady Macbeth mean when she says 'screw your courage to the sticking place and we'll not fail'?	
What happens in the opening scene of *Macbeth*?	
Who does Macbeth split open 'from the nave to the chops'?	
How does Lady Macbeth find out about the prophecy?	
Who is made heir to Duncan's throne in Act 1, Scene 4? What title does this character have?	
What does Macbeth feel about the plot to kill Duncan at the start of Act 1, Scene 7?	
What does Lady Macbeth mean when she says Macbeth is 'too full o' the milk of human kindness'?	
What are the three predictions made by the witches in Act 1, Scene 3?	
What does Macbeth mean when he says of Duncan that 'his virtues will plead like angels'?	
Who is at war with King Duncan when the play starts?	
What do Macbeth and Lady Macbeth decide to do in Act 1, Scene 5?	

Who does Macbeth split open 'from the nave to the chops'?	
Duncan's sons are called Malcolm and _____	
What do Macbeth and Lady Macbeth decide to do in Act 1, Scene 5?	
What does Lady Macbeth mean when she says 'screw your courage to the sticking place and we'll not fail'?	
Who is at war with King Duncan when the play starts?	
What are the three predictions made by the witches in Act 1, Scene 3?	
What does Lady Macbeth mean when she says Macbeth is 'too full o' the milk of human kindness'?	
What does Macbeth mean when he says of Duncan that 'his virtues will plead like angels'?	
What happens in the opening scene of *Macbeth*?	
Who is made heir to Duncan's throne in Act 1, Scene 4? What title does this character have?	
How does Lady Macbeth find out about the prophecy?	
What does Macbeth feel about the plot to kill Duncan at the start of Act 1, Scene 7?	

What does Macbeth mean when he says of Duncan that 'his virtues will plead like angels'?	
What happens in the opening scene of *Macbeth*?	
Who is made heir to Duncan's throne in Act 1, Scene 4? What title does this character have?	
Duncan's sons are called Malcolm and _____	
Who is at war with King Duncan when the play starts?	
What do Macbeth and Lady Macbeth decide to do in Act 1, Scene 5?	
How does Lady Macbeth find out about the prophecy?	
What does Macbeth feel about the plot to kill Duncan at the start of Act 1, Scene 7?	
What does Lady Macbeth mean when she says Macbeth is 'too full o' the milk of human kindness'?	
What does Lady Macbeth mean when she says 'screw your courage to the sticking place and we'll not fail'?	
Who does Macbeth split open 'from the nave to the chops'?	
What are the three predictions made by the witches in Act 1, Scene 3?	

ANSWER KEY

2.1	At the start of Act 2, why has Banquo been unable to sleep?	He has been dreaming of the 'weird sisters', the three witches
2.2	What is happening when Macbeth describes a 'false creation proceeding from the heat-oppressed brain'?	Macbeth has a vision of a dagger and he doesn't know if it is real, or whether the stress and guilt of the plan to murder Duncan is making him hallucinate
2.3	Why don't Duncan's guards wake up?	Lady Macbeth has drugged them so that they stay asleep
2.4	What does Macbeth mean when he says, 'Will all great Neptune's ocean wash this blood/Clean from my hand?'	He means that all the water in the world will never take away his guilt for murdering his king
2.5	What does Lady Macbeth do with the bloody daggers? Why?	She wipes blood on the guards while they are asleep and leaves the daggers with them, so that people will think they killed Duncan
2.6	Why does Lady Macbeth say she can't kill the king herself?	She says he looks like her father
2.7	Name three strange events on the night of Duncan's murder	1. Solar eclipse 2. Horses eat each other 3. Earthquake
2.8	What role does the Porter play in the structure of the drama?	He is the comic relief, providing a funny scene to lighten the violence and give the audience a rest. He also introduces the idea that the gates to Macbeth's home are like the gates of hell
2.9	Who does the Porter hear knocking at the door?	Lennox and Macduff
2.10	What does Macbeth do when everyone discovers Duncan is dead?	He kills the guards and claims that he did it because of anger
2.11	What do Malcolm and Donalbain do when they discover their father has been murdered?	They flee. Malcolm goes to England and Donalbain goes to Ireland
2.12	Where is Macbeth crowned king?	Scone

TRACKER

Quiz	Date	Score
1		
2		
3		
4		
5		
6		

Got it? ☐

2.1	At the start of Act 2, why has Banquo been unable to sleep?	
2.2	What is happening when Macbeth describes a 'false creation proceeding from the heat-oppressed brain'?	
2.3	Why don't Duncan's guards wake up?	
2.4	What does Macbeth mean when he says, 'Will all great Neptune's ocean wash this blood/Clean from my hand?'	
2.5	What does Lady Macbeth do with the bloody daggers? Why?	
2.6	Why does Lady Macbeth say she can't kill the king herself?	
2.7	Name three strange events on the night of Duncan's murder	
2.8	What role does the Porter play in the structure of the drama?	
2.9	Who does the Porter hear knocking at the door?	
2.10	What does Macbeth do when everyone discovers Duncan is dead?	
2.11	What do Malcolm and Donalbain do when they discover their father has been murdered?	
2.12	Where is Macbeth crowned king?	

Why don't Duncan's guards wake up?	
Why does Lady Macbeth say she can't kill the king herself?	
Who does the Porter hear knocking at the door?	
Where is Macbeth crowned king?	
What is happening when Macbeth describes a 'false creation proceeding from the heat-oppressed brain'?	
What does Macbeth mean when he says, 'Will all great Neptune's ocean wash this blood/Clean from my hand?'	
What role does the Porter play in the structure of the drama?	
What does Macbeth do when everyone discovers Duncan is dead?	
At the start of Act 2, why has Banquo been unable to sleep?	
What does Lady Macbeth do with the bloody daggers? Why?	
Name three strange events on the night of Duncan's murder	
What do Malcolm and Donalbain do when they discover their father has been murdered?	

Quiz 2: Act 2

What does Macbeth do when everyone discovers Duncan is dead?	
At the start of Act 2, why has Banquo been unable to sleep?	
What does Lady Macbeth do with the bloody daggers? Why?	
Why does Lady Macbeth say she can't kill the king herself?	
What is happening when Macbeth describes a 'false creation proceeding from the heat-oppressed brain'?	
Who does the Porter hear knocking at the door?	
Name three strange events on the night of Duncan's murder	
What do Malcolm and Donalbain do when they discover their father has been murdered?	
What role does the Porter play in the structure of the drama?	
Where is Macbeth crowned king?	
Why don't Duncan's guards wake up?	
What does Macbeth mean when he says, 'Will all great Neptune's ocean wash this blood/Clean from my hand?'	

Why does Lady Macbeth say she can't kill the king herself?	
Where is Macbeth crowned king?	
At the start of Act 2, why has Banquo been unable to sleep?	
Why don't Duncan's guards wake up?	
Name three strange events on the night of Duncan's murder	
What does Lady Macbeth do with the bloody daggers? Why?	
What do Malcolm and Donalbain do when they discover their father has been murdered?	
What role does the Porter play in the structure of the drama?	
What does Macbeth mean when he says, 'Will all great Neptune's ocean wash this blood/Clean from my hand?'	
What does Macbeth do when everyone discovers Duncan is dead?	
What is happening when Macbeth describes a 'false creation proceeding from the heat-oppressed brain'?	
Who does the Porter hear knocking at the door?	

Why don't Duncan's guards wake up?	
Why does Lady Macbeth say she can't kill the king herself?	
Who does the Porter hear knocking at the door?	
Where is Macbeth crowned king?	
What is happening when Macbeth describes a 'false creation proceeding from the heat-oppressed brain'?	
What does Macbeth mean when he says, 'Will all great Neptune's ocean wash this blood/Clean from my hand?'	
What role does the Porter play in the structure of the drama?	
What does Macbeth do when everyone discovers Duncan is dead?	
At the start of Act 2, why has Banquo been unable to sleep?	
What does Lady Macbeth do with the bloody daggers? Why?	
Name three strange events on the night of Duncan's murder	
What do Malcolm and Donalbain do when they discover their father has been murdered?	

What does Macbeth do when everyone discovers Duncan is dead?	
At the start of Act 2, why has Banquo been unable to sleep?	
What does Lady Macbeth do with the bloody daggers? Why?	
Why does Lady Macbeth say she can't kill the king herself?	
What is happening when Macbeth describes a 'false creation proceeding from the heat-oppressed brain'?	
Who does the Porter hear knocking at the door?	
Name three strange events on the night of Duncan's murder	
What do Malcolm and Donalbain do when they discover their father has been murdered?	
What role does the Porter play in the structure of the drama?	
Where is Macbeth crowned king?	
Why don't Duncan's guards wake up?	
What does Macbeth mean when he says, 'Will all great Neptune's ocean wash this blood/Clean from my hand?'	

ANSWER KEY

3.1	At the start of Act 3, what does Banquo mean when he says, 'May they not be my oracles as well/And set me up in hope?'	He is remembering the witches' prophecy and wonders whether he should be hopeful that his descendants will become kings
3.2	Why is Macbeth concerned about Banquo at the start of Act 3?	The witches prophesied that Banquo's sons would be kings, which is a threat to Macbeth's position
3.3	What is the name of Banquo's son?	Fleance
3.4	What happens to Banquo and his son?	Macbeth hires assassins to kill them. Banquo is killed but Fleance escapes
3.5	Who is at the banquet?	Macbeth, Lady Macbeth, Lennox, Ross and the other lords
3.6	What happens at the banquet?	The ghost of Banquo appears but only Macbeth can see it. Macbeth reacts with a mixture of terror and bravado, but it all looks very odd to the other guests
3.7	What does Lady Macbeth do in response to Macbeth's behaviour at the banquet?	She tells the guests not to worry and that Macbeth has had visions since he was young. Later, when Macbeth appears to be getting worse, she asks the guests to leave
3.8	What does Macbeth decide to do after the guests have left the banquet?	He is worried about Macduff's loyalty and considering killing him. He decides to go to the witches again to see what they will say
3.9	What do the witches decide in Act 3, Scene 5?	They will meet Macbeth and trick him with visions and spirits
3.10	Why does Macbeth begin to prepare for war?	He has heard that Malcolm and Macduff have gone to England to ask King Edward for help
3.11	Who is blamed for Banquo's murder?	Fleance
3.12	Why do Lennox and the Lord call Macbeth a 'tyrant'?	They believe he has murdered Duncan and Banquo. They hope that Scotland can be saved from Macbeth

TRACKER

Quiz	Date	Score
1		
2		
3		
4		
5		
6		

Got it? ☐

3.1	At the start of Act 3, what does Banquo mean when he says, 'May they not be my oracles as well/And set me up in hope?'	
3.2	Why is Macbeth concerned about Banquo at the start of Act 3?	
3.3	What is the name of Banquo's son?	
3.4	What happens to Banquo and his son?	
3.5	Who is at the banquet?	
3.6	What happens at the banquet?	
3.7	What does Lady Macbeth do in response to Macbeth's behaviour at the banquet?	
3.8	What does Macbeth decide to do after the guests have left the banquet?	
3.9	What do the witches decide in Act 3, Scene 5?	
3.10	Why does Macbeth begin to prepare for war?	
3.11	Who is blamed for Banquo's murder?	
3.12	Why do Lennox and the Lord call Macbeth a 'tyrant'?	

What is the name of Banquo's son?	
What happens at the banquet?	
What do the witches decide in Act 3, Scene 5?	
Why do Lennox and the Lord call Macbeth a 'tyrant'?	
Why is Macbeth concerned about Banquo at the start of Act 3?	
What happens to Banquo and his son?	
What does Macbeth decide to do after the guests have left the banquet?	
Why does Macbeth begin to prepare for war?	
At the start of Act 3, what does Banquo mean when he says, 'May they not be my oracles as well/And set me up in hope?'	
Who is at the banquet?	
What does Lady Macbeth do in response to Macbeth's behaviour at the banquet?	
Who is blamed for Banquo's murder?	

Why does Macbeth begin to prepare for war?	
At the start of Act 3, what does Banquo mean when he says, 'May they not be my oracles as well/And set me up in hope?'	
Who is at the banquet?	
What happens at the banquet?	
Why is Macbeth concerned about Banquo at the start of Act 3?	
What do the witches decide in Act 3, Scene 5?	
What does Lady Macbeth do in response to Macbeth's behaviour at the banquet?	
Who is blamed for Banquo's murder?	
What does Macbeth decide to do after the guests have left the banquet?	
Why do Lennox and the Lord call Macbeth a 'tyrant'?	
What is the name of Banquo's son?	
What happens to Banquo and his son?	

What happens at the banquet?	
Why do Lennox and the Lord call Macbeth a 'tyrant'?	
At the start of Act 3, what does Banquo mean when he says, 'May they not be my oracles as well/And set me up in hope?'	
What is the name of Banquo's son?	
What does Lady Macbeth do in response to Macbeth's behaviour at the banquet?	
Who is at the banquet?	
Who is blamed for Banquo's murder?	
What does Macbeth decide to do after the guests have left the banquet?	
What happens to Banquo and his son?	
Why does Macbeth begin to prepare for war?	
Why is Macbeth concerned about Banquo at the start of Act 3?	
What do the witches decide in Act 3, Scene 5?	

What is the name of Banquo's son?	
What happens at the banquet?	
What do the witches decide in Act 3, Scene 5?	
Why do Lennox and the Lord call Macbeth a 'tyrant'?	
Why is Macbeth concerned about Banquo at the start of Act 3?	
What happens to Banquo and his son?	
What does Macbeth decide to do after the guests have left the banquet?	
Why does Macbeth begin to prepare for war?	
At the start of Act 3, what does Banquo mean when he says, 'May they not be my oracles as well/And set me up in hope?'	
Who is at the banquet?	
What does Lady Macbeth do in response to Macbeth's behaviour at the banquet?	
Who is blamed for Banquo's murder?	

Why does Macbeth begin to prepare for war?	
At the start of Act 3, what does Banquo mean when he says, 'May they not be my oracles as well/And set me up in hope?'	
Who is at the banquet?	
What happens at the banquet?	
Why is Macbeth concerned about Banquo at the start of Act 3?	
What do the witches decide in Act 3, Scene 5?	
What does Lady Macbeth do in response to Macbeth's behaviour at the banquet?	
Who is blamed for Banquo's murder?	
What does Macbeth decide to do after the guests have left the banquet?	
Why do Lennox and the Lord call Macbeth a 'tyrant'?	
What is the name of Banquo's son?	
What happens to Banquo and his son?	

ANSWER KEY

4.1	What are the witches doing at the start of Act 4?	They are circling a cauldron and chanting spells while adding strange ingredients to the pot
4.2	What happens when the witches say, 'By the pricking of my thumbs/Something wicked this way comes'?	Macbeth enters
4.3	What does Macbeth ask the witches?	He asks them to tell him the truth about their predictions
4.4	What are the apparitions?	• Macduff • A bloody child • A child with a crown and a tree • A parade of eight kings • Banquo's ghost
4.5	What is Macbeth told by the witches?	• Beware of Macduff • No man born of woman may kill Macbeth • Macbeth will not be beaten until Birnam Wood marches to Dunsinane Hill
4.6	What does Macbeth do to Macduff?	He has his wife and children murdered in their castle
4.7	Why does Lady Macduff feel betrayed?	Her husband has gone to England, leaving her and the children alone and in danger
4.8	Why is Malcolm unsure about whether to trust Macduff?	Because Macduff has left his family in Scotland – Malcolm thinks Macduff may be working for Macbeth
4.9	Why does Malcolm talk about his sexual desires and vices?	He is testing Macduff to see if he is an honest, trustworthy man
4.10	What does Ross say to Malcolm when Ross first arrives in England?	He begs Malcolm to come back to Scotland and defeat Macbeth
4.11	What does Macduff mean when he says, 'All my pretty ones? Did you say all?'	Have all of my children been killed?
4.12	What does Malcolm say to Macduff at the end of Act 4?	He promises that they will have revenge on Macbeth

TRACKER

Quiz	Date	Score
1		
2		
3		
4		
5		
6		

Got it? ☐

4.1	What are the witches doing at the start of Act 4?	
4.2	What happens when the witches say, 'By the pricking of my thumbs/Something wicked this way comes'?	
4.3	What does Macbeth ask the witches?	
4.4	What are the apparitions?	
4.5	What is Macbeth told by the witches?	
4.6	What does Macbeth do to Macduff?	
4.7	Why does Lady Macduff feel betrayed?	
4.8	Why is Malcolm unsure about whether to trust Macduff?	
4.9	Why does Malcolm talk about his sexual desires and vices?	
4.10	What does Ross say to Malcolm when Ross first arrives in England?	
4.11	What does Macduff mean when he says, 'All my pretty ones? Did you say all?'	
4.12	What does Malcolm say to Macduff at the end of Act 4?	

What does Macbeth ask the witches?	
What does Macbeth do to Macduff?	
Why does Malcolm talk about his sexual desires and vices?	
What does Malcolm say to Macduff at the end of Act 4?	
What happens when the witches say, 'By the pricking of my thumbs/Something wicked this way comes'?	
What are the apparitions?	
Why is Malcolm unsure about whether to trust Macduff?	
What does Ross say to Malcolm when Ross first arrives in England?	
What are the witches doing at the start of Act 4?	
What is Macbeth told by the witches?	
Why does Lady Macduff feel betrayed?	
What does Macduff mean when he says, 'All my pretty ones? Did you say all?'	

Quiz 4: Act 4

What does Ross say to Malcolm when Ross first arrives in England?	
What are the witches doing at the start of Act 4?	
What is Macbeth told by the witches?	
What does Macbeth do to Macduff?	
What happens when the witches say, 'By the pricking of my thumbs/Something wicked this way comes'?	
Why does Malcolm talk about his sexual desires and vices?	
Why does Lady Macduff feel betrayed?	
What does Macduff mean when he says, 'All my pretty ones? Did you say all?'	
Why is Malcolm unsure about whether to trust Macduff?	
What does Malcolm say to Macduff at the end of Act 4?	
What does Macbeth ask the witches?	
What are the apparitions?	

What does Macbeth do to Macduff?	
What does Malcolm say to Macduff at the end of Act 4?	
What are the witches doing at the start of Act 4?	
What does Macbeth ask the witches?	
Why does Lady Macduff feel betrayed?	
What is Macbeth told by the witches?	
What does Macduff mean when he says, 'All my pretty ones? Did you say all?'	
Why is Malcolm unsure about whether to trust Macduff?	
What are the apparitions?	
What does Ross say to Malcolm when Ross first arrives in England?	
What happens when the witches say, 'By the pricking of my thumbs/Something wicked this way comes'?	
Why does Malcolm talk about his sexual desires and vices?	

What does Macbeth ask the witches?	
What does Macbeth do to Macduff?	
Why does Malcolm talk about his sexual desires and vices?	
What does Malcolm say to Macduff at the end of Act 4?	
What happens when the witches say, 'By the pricking of my thumbs/Something wicked this way comes'?	
What are the apparitions?	
Why is Malcolm unsure about whether to trust Macduff?	
What does Ross say to Malcolm when Ross first arrives in England?	
What are the witches doing at the start of Act 4?	
What is Macbeth told by the witches?	
Why does Lady Macduff feel betrayed?	
What does Macduff mean when he says, 'All my pretty ones? Did you say all?'	

What does Ross say to Malcolm when Ross first arrives in England?	
What are the witches doing at the start of Act 4?	
What is Macbeth told by the witches?	
What does Macbeth do to Macduff?	
What happens when the witches say, 'By the pricking of my thumbs/Something wicked this way comes'?	
Why does Malcolm talk about his sexual desires and vices?	
Why does Lady Macduff feel betrayed?	
What does Macduff mean when he says, 'All my pretty ones? Did you say all?'	
Why is Malcolm unsure about whether to trust Macduff?	
What does Malcolm say to Macduff at the end of Act 4?	
What does Macbeth ask the witches?	
What are the apparitions?	

ANSWER KEY

5.1	What is Lady Macbeth doing at the start of Act 5?	She is sleepwalking and talking to herself. She keeps washing her hands and talking about Duncan's murder
5.2	Who is with Lady Macbeth at the start of Act 5?	A doctor and a gentlewoman are observing her
5.3	Who is Lord Siward?	An English lord who has brought the English army to support the Scottish army led by Malcolm
5.4	Where are the English and Scottish armies at the start of Act 5?	The armies are both close by and are going to meet at Birnam Wood. Macbeth is waiting in Dunsinane Castle, preparing for battle
5.5	Why is Macbeth confident that he will win the battle?	Because he believes that no man born of woman can kill him, and that he can't be defeated until Birnam Wood comes to Dunsinane Hill
5.6	What do Macbeth and the Doctor discuss about Lady Macbeth?	She is having trouble sleeping and is experiencing visions. Macbeth tells the Doctor to cure her with medicine
5.7	How do Malcolm's soldiers plan to disguise their numbers?	Each soldier will carry a tree branch in front of him as the army marches
5.8	What does it mean that Birnam Wood comes to Dunsinane?	Because the soldiers are all carrying branches from trees, it looks as though the forest is moving as they march
5.9	Why does Macbeth say, 'Out, out, brief candle'?	He has heard that Lady Macbeth is dead. He says that all life is short and has no meaning
5.10	What does Macbeth learn when he meets Macduff on the battlefield?	Macduff was born by caesarean section, so he was not 'born of woman'
5.11	How does Macbeth die?	Macduff defeats and beheads him
5.12	What does Malcolm do as his first act of kingship?	He declares that all his thanes will be made earls – like in the English peerage system

TRACKER

Quiz	Date	Score
1		
2		
3		
4		
5		
6		

Got it? ☐

Quiz 5: Act 5

5.1	What is Lady Macbeth doing at the start of Act 5?	
5.2	Who is with Lady Macbeth at the start of Act 5?	
5.3	Who is Lord Siward?	
5.4	Where are the English and Scottish armies at the start of Act 5?	
5.5	Why is Macbeth confident that he will win the battle?	
5.6	What do Macbeth and the Doctor discuss about Lady Macbeth?	
5.7	How do Malcolm's soldiers plan to disguise their numbers?	
5.8	What does it mean that Birnam Wood comes to Dunsinane?	
5.9	Why does Macbeth say, 'Out, out, brief candle'?	
5.10	What does Macbeth learn when he meets Macduff on the battlefield?	
5.11	How does Macbeth die?	
5.12	What does Malcolm do as his first act of kingship?	

Who is Lord Siward?	
What do Macbeth and the Doctor discuss about Lady Macbeth?	
Why does Macbeth say, 'Out, out, brief candle'?	
What does Malcolm do as his first act of kingship?	
Who is with Lady Macbeth at the start of Act 5?	
Where are the English and Scottish armies at the start of Act 5?	
What does it mean that Birnam Wood comes to Dunsinane?	
What does Macbeth learn when he meets Macduff on the battlefield?	
What is Lady Macbeth doing at the start of Act 5?	
Why is Macbeth confident that he will win the battle?	
How do Malcolm's soldiers plan to disguise their numbers?	
How does Macbeth die?	

What does Macbeth learn when he meets Macduff on the battlefield?	
What is Lady Macbeth doing at the start of Act 5?	
Why is Macbeth confident that he will win the battle?	
What do Macbeth and the Doctor discuss about Lady Macbeth?	
Who is with Lady Macbeth at the start of Act 5?	
Why does Macbeth say, 'Out, out, brief candle'?	
How do Malcolm's soldiers plan to disguise their numbers?	
How does Macbeth die?	
What does it mean that Birnam Wood comes to Dunsinane?	
What does Malcolm do as his first act of kingship?	
Who is Lord Siward?	
Where are the English and Scottish armies at the start of Act 5?	

What do Macbeth and the Doctor discuss about Lady Macbeth?	
What does Malcolm do as his first act of kingship?	
What is Lady Macbeth doing at the start of Act 5?	
Who is Lord Siward?	
How do Malcolm's soldiers plan to disguise their numbers?	
Why is Macbeth confident that he will win the battle?	
How does Macbeth die?	
What does it mean that Birnam Wood comes to Dunsinane?	
Where are the English and Scottish armies at the start of Act 5?	
What does Macbeth learn when he meets Macduff on the battlefield?	
Who is with Lady Macbeth at the start of Act 5?	
Why does Macbeth say, 'Out, out, brief candle'?	

Who is Lord Siward?	
What do Macbeth and the Doctor discuss about Lady Macbeth?	
Why does Macbeth say, 'Out, out, brief candle'?	
What does Malcolm do as his first act of kingship?	
Who is with Lady Macbeth at the start of Act 5?	
Where are the English and Scottish armies at the start of Act 5?	
What does it mean that Birnam Wood comes to Dunsinane?	
What does Macbeth learn when he meets Macduff on the battlefield?	
What is Lady Macbeth doing at the start of Act 5?	
Why is Macbeth confident that he will win the battle?	
How do Malcolm's soldiers plan to disguise their numbers?	
How does Macbeth die?	

What does Macbeth learn when he meets Macduff on the battlefield?	
What is Lady Macbeth doing at the start of Act 5?	
Why is Macbeth confident that he will win the battle?	
What do Macbeth and the Doctor discuss about Lady Macbeth?	
Who is with Lady Macbeth at the start of Act 5?	
Why does Macbeth say, 'Out, out, brief candle'?	
How do Malcolm's soldiers plan to disguise their numbers?	
How does Macbeth die?	
What does it mean that Birnam Wood comes to Dunsinane?	
What does Malcolm do as his first act of kingship?	
Who is Lord Siward?	
Where are the English and Scottish armies at the start of Act 5?	

Context

ANSWER KEY

6.1	When is it thought that *Macbeth* was first performed?	1606
6.2	When was *Macbeth* first published?	1623
6.3	What was one of Shakespeare's historical sources for the story of Macbeth?	*Holinshed's Chronicles* (1587) includes an account of the lives of Macbeth, Macduff and Duncan
6.4	What genre of play is *Macbeth*?	A tragedy with some elements of history
6.5	Why do some people call *Macbeth* 'the Scottish play'?	Some people in the theatre world think the play is cursed and will not say its name out loud
6.6	Who was the real Macbeth?	A king who ruled Scotland for 17 years from 1040. Unlike Shakespeare's Macbeth, the real Macbeth succeeded to the throne after Duncan was killed in battle and he had a mostly peaceful reign
6.7	Why was *Macbeth* written?	It was a tribute to James I, the new king of England
6.8	Which elements of *Macbeth* would have particularly appealed to James I?	• Witchcraft: he wrote *Daemonologie* and was interested in magic • Lineage: James believed he was a descendant of Banquo
6.9	Aside from Banquo, what are some other examples of ghosts in Shakespeare plays?	Ghosts in Shakespeare are always the spirits of people who have been murdered: • *Hamlet*: the ghost of Hamlet's father • *Julius Caesar*: the ghost of Caesar • *Richard III*: the ghosts of Henry VI and Edward IV
6.10	Name some other Shakespeare plays that explore the idea that human wickedness is reflected in turmoil in the natural world (i.e. storms to reflect tragedy)	• *King Lear*: storm on the heath after Lear has been cast out by his daughters • *Julius Caesar*: storm in Rome before the assassination of Caesar

TRACKER

Quiz	Date	Score
1		
2		
3		
4		
5		
6		

Got it? ☐

6.1	When is it thought that *Macbeth* was first performed?	
6.2	When was *Macbeth* first published?	
6.3	What was one of Shakespeare's historical sources for the story of Macbeth?	
6.4	What genre of play is *Macbeth*?	
6.5	Why do some people call *Macbeth* 'the Scottish play'?	
6.6	Who was the real Macbeth?	
6.7	Why was *Macbeth* written?	
6.8	Which elements of *Macbeth* would have particularly appealed to James I?	
6.9	Aside from Banquo, what are some other examples of ghosts in Shakespeare plays?	
6.10	Name some other Shakespeare plays that explore the idea that human wickedness is reflected in turmoil in the natural world (i.e. storms to reflect tragedy)	

What was one of Shakespeare's historical sources for the story of Macbeth?	
Who was the real Macbeth?	
Aside from Banquo, what are some other examples of ghosts in Shakespeare plays?	
When was *Macbeth* first published?	
What genre of play is *Macbeth*?	
Which elements of *Macbeth* would have particularly appealed to James I?	
Name some other Shakespeare plays that explore the idea that human wickedness is reflected in turmoil in the natural world (i.e. storms to reflect tragedy)	
When is it thought that *Macbeth* was first performed?	
Why do some people call *Macbeth* 'the Scottish play'?	
Why was *Macbeth* written?	

Name some other Shakespeare plays that explore the idea that human wickedness is reflected in turmoil in the natural world (i.e. storms to reflect tragedy)	
When is it thought that *Macbeth* was first performed?	
Why do some people call *Macbeth* 'the Scottish play'?	
Who was the real Macbeth?	
When was *Macbeth* first published?	
Aside from Banquo, what are some other examples of ghosts in Shakespeare plays?	
Why was *Macbeth* written?	
Which elements of *Macbeth* would have particularly appealed to James I?	
What was one of Shakespeare's historical sources for the story of Macbeth?	
What genre of play is *Macbeth*?	

Who was the real Macbeth?	
When is it thought that *Macbeth* was first performed?	
What was one of Shakespeare's historical sources for the story of Macbeth?	
Why was *Macbeth* written?	
Why do some people call *Macbeth* 'the Scottish play'?	
Which elements of *Macbeth* would have particularly appealed to James I?	
What genre of play is *Macbeth*?	
Name some other Shakespeare plays that explore the idea that human wickedness is reflected in turmoil in the natural world (i.e. storms to reflect tragedy)	
When was *Macbeth* first published?	
Aside from Banquo, what are some other examples of ghosts in Shakespeare plays?	

What was one of Shakespeare's historical sources for the story of Macbeth?	
Who was the real Macbeth?	
Aside from Banquo, what are some other examples of ghosts in Shakespeare plays?	
When was *Macbeth* first published?	
What genre of play is *Macbeth*?	
Which elements of *Macbeth* would have particularly appealed to James I?	
Name some other Shakespeare plays that explore the idea that human wickedness is reflected in turmoil in the natural world (i.e. storms to reflect tragedy)	
When is it thought that *Macbeth* was first performed?	
Why do some people call *Macbeth* 'the Scottish play'?	
Why was *Macbeth* written?	

Name some other Shakespeare plays that explore the idea that human wickedness is reflected in turmoil in the natural world (i.e. storms to reflect tragedy)	
When is it thought that *Macbeth* was first performed?	
Why do some people call *Macbeth* 'the Scottish play'?	
Who was the real Macbeth?	
When was *Macbeth* first published?	
Aside from Banquo, what are some other examples of ghosts in Shakespeare plays?	
Why was *Macbeth* written?	
Which elements of *Macbeth* would have particularly appealed to James I?	
What was one of Shakespeare's historical sources for the story of Macbeth?	
What genre of play is *Macbeth*?	

ANSWER KEY

7.1	What is the divine right of kings?	The belief that kings and queens have a God-given right to rule and that rebellion against them is a sin
7.2	What is the Great Chain of Being?	The structure and hierarchy of all life and matter in the universe, starting with God at the top. By killing a king, Macbeth disrupts the Great Chain and society begins to crumble
7.3	What was the difference between a Catholic and a Protestant in Jacobean England?	Catholics and Protestants were both Christian, but they differed on key elements of doctrine. One of the main differences was that Catholics believed the Pope was the head of the church, but Protestants saw the king or queen as head of the church
7.4	How did England change from Catholic to Protestant?	England had gone through many years of religious turmoil. Henry VIII converted the country from Catholicism to Protestantism. His daughter Mary changed the national religion back to Catholicism and persecuted Protestants. Elizabeth I did the opposite and persecuted Catholics. Many people died because of their faith
7.5	Why did James VI of Scotland become the king of England?	Elizabeth I died childless. James was the son of Mary Queen of Scots and the great-great-grandson of Henry VII
7.6	What religion was James I?	He was Protestant. He enforced laws that persecuted Catholics
7.7	Which book did James I publish in 1597 (while he was still James VI of Scotland)?	*Daemonologie*, a book about the dangers of witchcraft
7.8	In 1603, which law was passed in parliament?	An anti-witchcraft law against any 'invocation or conjuration of any evil or wicked spirit'
7.9	What happened in 1605?	The Gunpowder Plot. A group of English Catholics attempted to assassinate James I by blowing up the House of Lords
7.10	How did James I react to the threats on his life?	He was extremely paranoid, and increased his persecution and oppression of Catholics
7.11	What is equivocation?	Equivocation is the use of ambiguous phrases in order to mislead people
7.12	How can *The Prince* by Machiavelli be linked to *Macbeth*?	*The Prince* is a book about political power that, among other things, argues that a successful leader should appear good to the public and keep his darker side hidden

TRACKER

Quiz	Date	Score
1		
2		
3		
4		
5		
6		

Got it? ☐

7.1	What is the divine right of kings?	
7.2	What is the Great Chain of Being?	
7.3	What was the difference between a Catholic and a Protestant in Jacobean England?	
7.4	How did England change from Catholic to Protestant?	
7.5	Why did James VI of Scotland become the king of England?	
7.6	What religion was James I?	
7.7	Which book did James I publish in 1597 (while he was still James VI of Scotland)?	
7.8	In 1603, which law was passed in parliament?	
7.9	What happened in 1605?	
7.10	How did James I react to the threats on his life?	
7.11	What is equivocation?	
7.12	How can *The Prince* by Machiavelli be linked to *Macbeth*?	

What was the difference between a Catholic and a Protestant in Jacobean England?	
What religion was James I?	
What happened in 1605?	
How can *The Prince* by Machiavelli be linked to *Macbeth*?	
What is the Great Chain of Being?	
How did England change from Catholic to Protestant?	
In 1603, which law was passed in parliament?	
How did James I react to the threats on his life?	
What is the divine right of kings?	
Why did James VI of Scotland become the king of England?	
Which book did James I publish in 1597 (while he was still James VI of Scotland)?	
What is equivocation?	

How did James I react to the threats on his life?	
What is the divine right of kings?	
Why did James VI of Scotland become the king of England?	
What religion was James I?	
What is the Great Chain of Being?	
What happened in 1605?	
Which book did James I publish in 1597 (while he was still James VI of Scotland)?	
What is equivocation?	
In 1603, which law was passed in parliament?	
How can *The Prince* by Machiavelli be linked to *Macbeth*?	
What was the difference between a Catholic and a Protestant in Jacobean England?	
How did England change from Catholic to Protestant?	

What religion was James I?	
How can *The Prince* by Machiavelli be linked to *Macbeth*?	
What is the divine right of kings?	
What was the difference between a Catholic and a Protestant in Jacobean England?	
Which book did James I publish in 1597 (while he was still James VI of Scotland)?	
Why did James VI of Scotland become the king of England?	
What is equivocation?	
In 1603, which law was passed in parliament?	
How did England change from Catholic to Protestant?	
How did James I react to the threats on his life?	
What is the Great Chain of Being?	
What happened in 1605?	

What was the difference between a Catholic and a Protestant in Jacobean England?	
What religion was James I?	
What happened in 1605?	
How can *The Prince* by Machiavelli be linked to *Macbeth*?	
What is the Great Chain of Being?	
How did England change from Catholic to Protestant?	
In 1603, which law was passed in parliament?	
How did James I react to the threats on his life?	
What is the divine right of kings?	
Why did James VI of Scotland become the king of England?	
Which book did James I publish in 1597 (while he was still James VI of Scotland)?	
What is equivocation?	

How did James I react to the threats on his life?	
What is the divine right of kings?	
Why did James VI of Scotland become the king of England?	
What religion was James I?	
What is the Great Chain of Being?	
What happened in 1605?	
Which book did James I publish in 1597 (while he was still James VI of Scotland)?	
What is equivocation?	
In 1603, which law was passed in parliament?	
How can *The Prince* by Machiavelli be linked to *Macbeth*?	
What was the difference between a Catholic and a Protestant in Jacobean England?	
How did England change from Catholic to Protestant?	

The next three quizzes explore some of the key influences in *Macbeth*. Influences are ideas that may have inspired or affected Shakespeare's writings. Understanding these influences will help you to develop your analysis and make more informed comments about context. For each one, try to memorise and complete the mind map.

The Oracle of Delphi

A high priestess in Greek legend who was believed to deliver prophecies inspired by the god Apollo. She famously gave advice that was ambiguous and misleading

The Fates

Three sisters who appear in many European mythologies (including Norse, Greek and Roman). They represent destiny and are depicted as having control over the lifespan of all mortals

Influences – the witches

Hecate

A goddess in Greek mythology associated with magic, witchcraft and ghosts. Most scholars believe that Shakespeare did not write the scene with Hecate, and that it was added later by someone else

Daemonologie

The book published by James I in 1597 – he was obsessed by witchcraft. The witches in *Macbeth* do many of the things described by James I, such as vanishing into thin air, raising storms, dancing and chanting, and performing sexual acts

TRACKER

Quiz	Date	Score
1		
2		
3		
4		
5		
6		

Got it? ☐

The Oracle of Delphi

The Fates

Influences – the witches

Hecate

Daemonologie

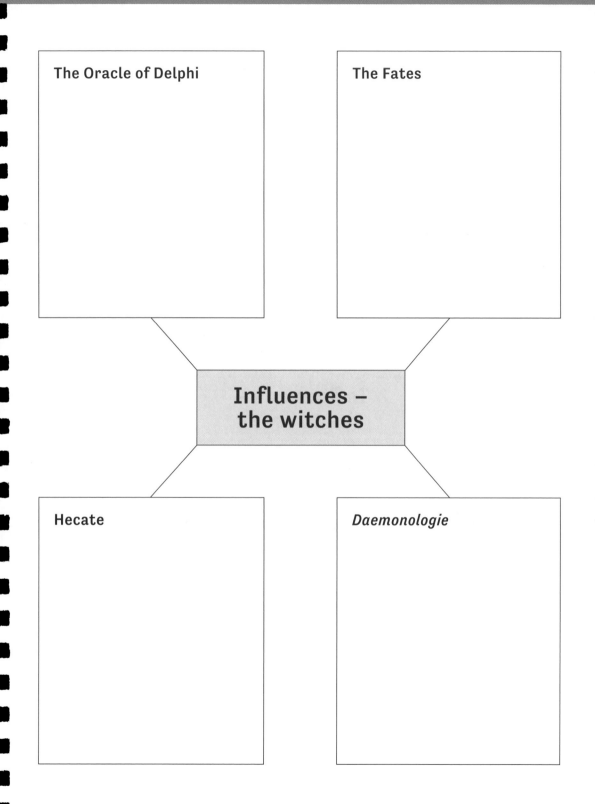

The Oracle of Delphi

The Fates

Influences –
the witches

Hecate

Daemonologie

The Oracle of Delphi

The Fates

Influences – the witches

Hecate

Daemonologie

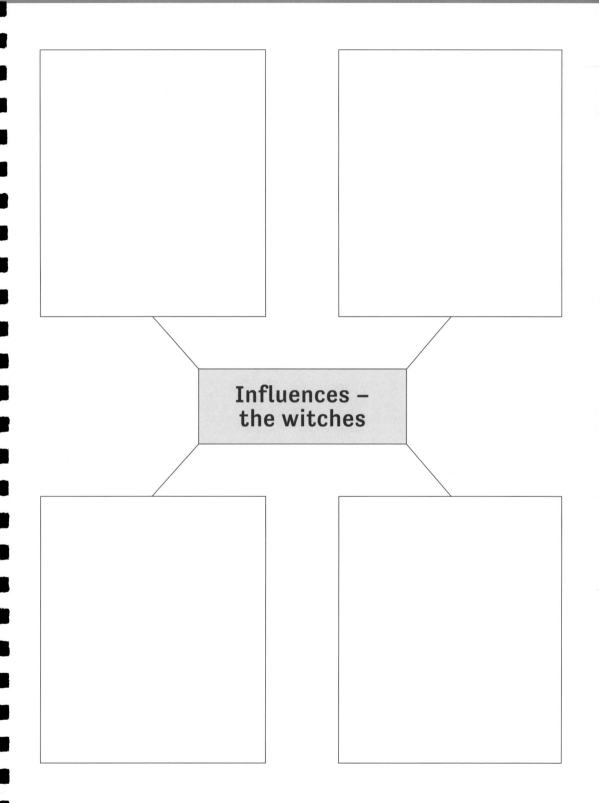

Influences –
the witches

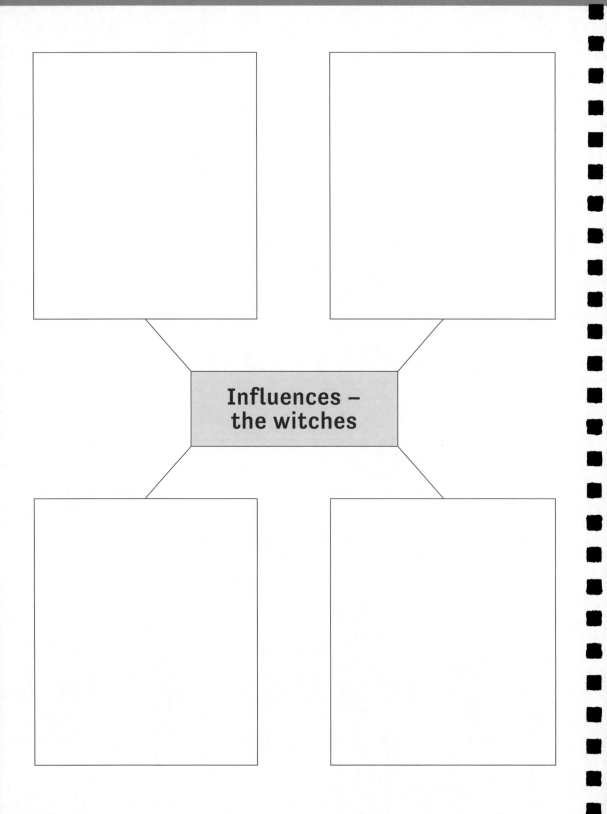

**Influences –
the witches**

Influences –
the witches

Washing hands: Pontius Pilate

In the Bible, Jesus was sentenced to death by Pontius Pilate. Pilate didn't want to do it, but he was forced to by the crowd. Afterwards, he washed his hands and said, 'I am innocent of the blood of this just man' (New Testament, Matthew 27)

Shedding blood

Macbeth says, 'It will have blood; they say blood will have blood' (3.4). The Bible is full of ideas about killing leading to more killing: 'Whoso sheddeth man's blood, by man shall his blood be shed' (Old Testament, Genesis 9)

Influences – blood

Bloody hands in Shakespeare

There are other images of bloody hands in Shakespeare plays – for example, in *Julius Caesar*, the murderers say 'let us bathe our hands in Caesar's blood'. Bloody hands are a symbol of guilt throughout literature

Golgotha

At the start of *Macbeth*, the Sergeant talks about bleeding wounds and describes the battle as 'another Golgotha'. In the Bible, when Jesus dies, a Roman soldier pierces Jesus's side with a spear as he hangs from the cross. Golgotha is the name of the place where Jesus is crucified and this is where his blood is spilled on the ground

TRACKER

Quiz	Date	Score
1		
2		
3		
4		
5		
6		

Got it? ☐

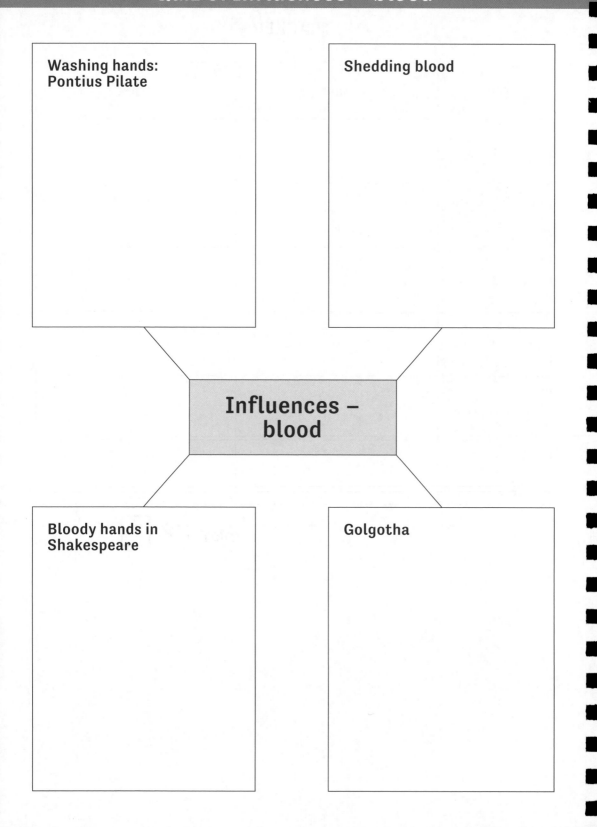

**Washing hands:
Pontius Pilate**

Shedding blood

Influences – blood

**Bloody hands in
Shakespeare**

Golgotha

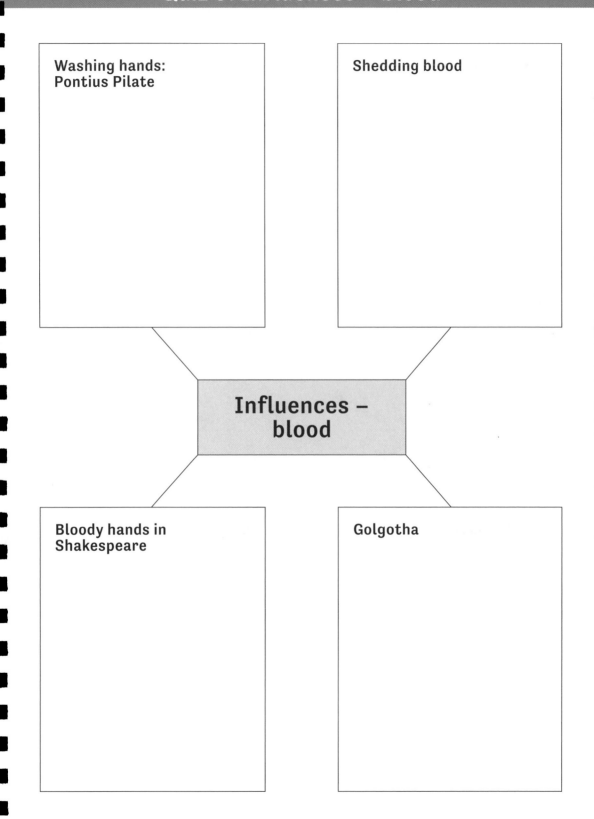

Washing hands:
Pontius Pilate

Shedding blood

Influences –
blood

Bloody hands in
Shakespeare

Golgotha

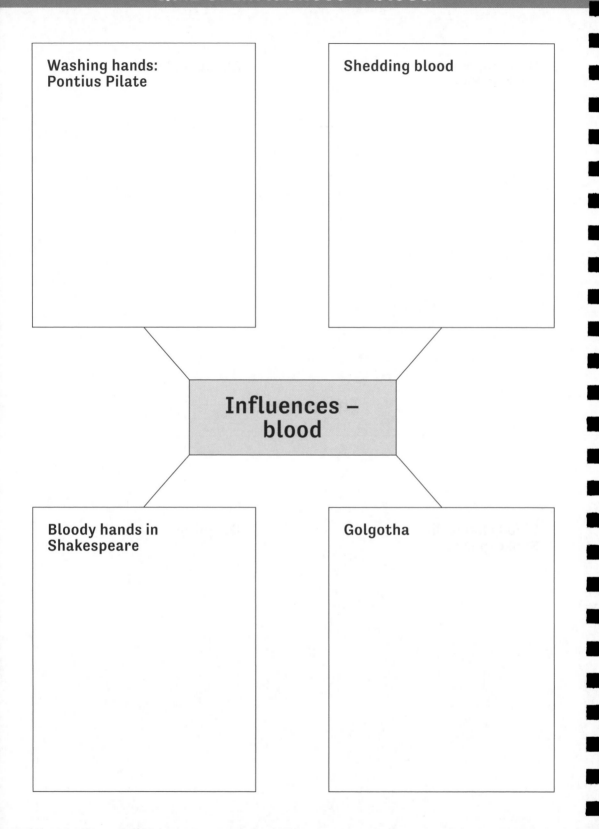

Washing hands:
Pontius Pilate

Shedding blood

Influences – blood

Bloody hands in
Shakespeare

Golgotha

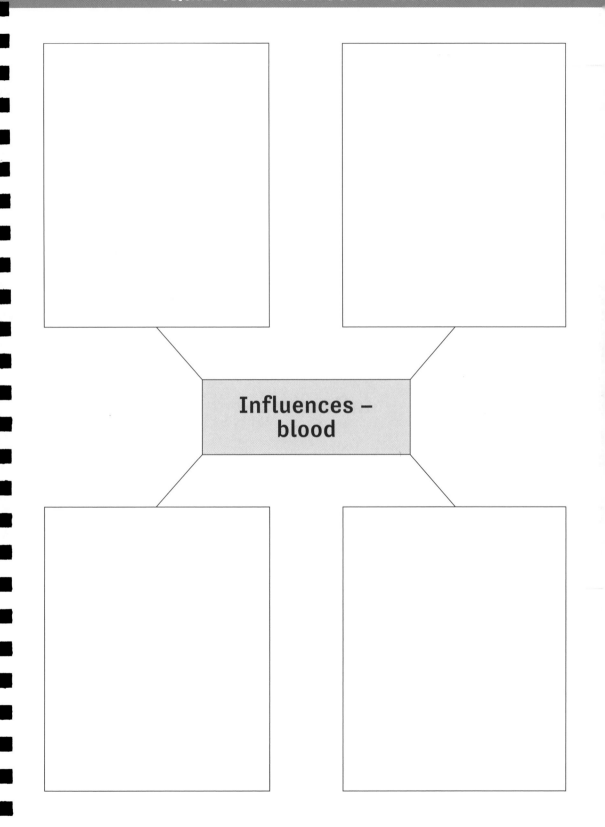

Influences –
blood

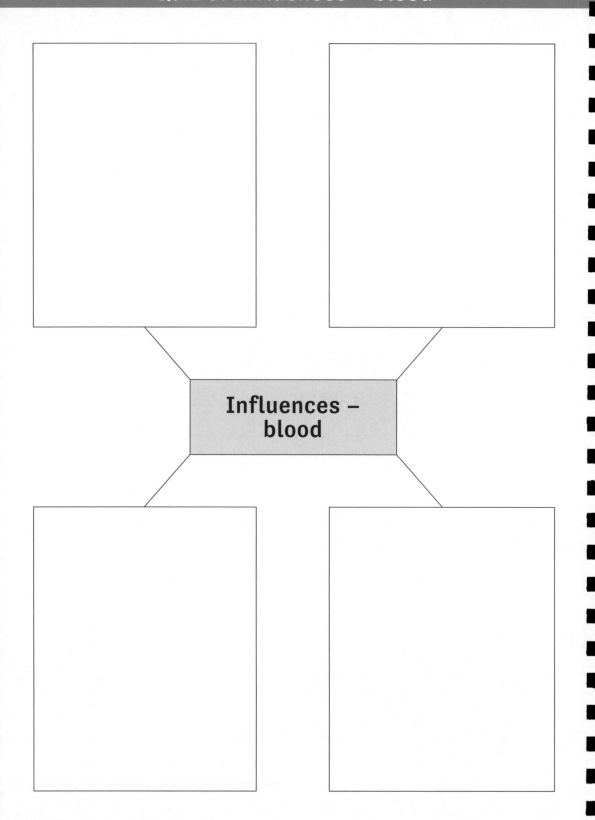

Influences – blood

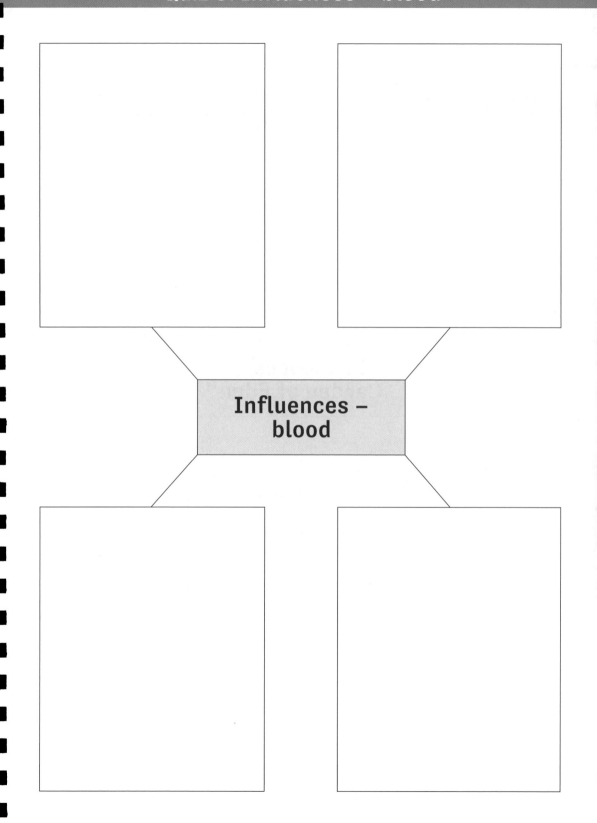

Influences –
blood

Breaking God's law

In the Garden of Eden story, Adam and Eve are told not to eat from the Tree of Knowledge. They break this commandment and are thrown out of the garden. Macbeth and Lady Macbeth also break God's law by killing a king, and they are punished for it

Snakes

The serpent in the Garden of Eden is the devil in disguise. This lying snake is used in imagery throughout literature. In *Macbeth*, Lady Macbeth encourages her husband to pretend to be loyal to Duncan: 'Look like the innocent flower/But be the serpent under't'

Influences – Garden of Eden

Women as temptresses

In the Garden of Eden story, Eve is persuaded by a serpent that she should eat the fruit. She then convinces Adam to break God's law. Lady Macbeth similarly convinces Macbeth to kill Duncan. Both women are seen as temptresses who lead men astray

Quiz 10: Influences – Garden of Eden

TRACKER

Quiz	Date	Score
1		
2		
3		
4		
5		
6		

Got it? ☐

Breaking God's law

Snakes

Influences – Garden of Eden

Women as temptresses

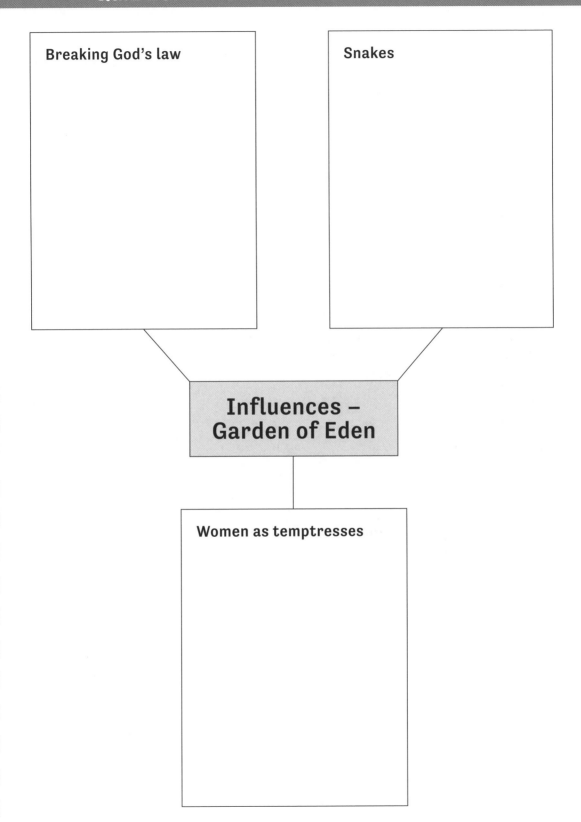

Breaking God's law

Snakes

Influences – Garden of Eden

Women as temptresses

Breaking God's law

Snakes

Influences – Garden of Eden

Women as temptresses

**Influences –
Garden of Eden**

**Influences –
Garden of Eden**

**Influences –
Garden of Eden**

Key term definitions and spellings

You need to mention the technical devices used by writers in your literature responses. All the devices mentioned in the next four quizzes can be found in *Macbeth*. Once you have learned what they are, you could improve your revision by finding examples of them in the play.

Quiz 11: Key term definitions 1

ANSWER KEY

	Terms	Definitions
11.1	Iambic pentameter	A metre in poetry with five iambs and 10 syllables per line (di-dum, di-dum, di-dum, di-dum, di-dum)
11.2	Blank verse	Poetry written in iambic pentameter that doesn't rhyme
11.3	Couplet	A pair of lines that rhyme with each other
11.4	Rhythm	A regular repeated pattern of stressed or unstressed syllables
11.5	Metre	The rhythm of a piece of poetry
11.6	Soliloquy	A speech in a play that a character delivers to herself/himself or to the audience, rather than to other characters
11.7	Aside	A remark made in a play that is only supposed to be heard by the audience
11.8	Dramatic irony	Where the audience understands the irony of the situation on stage, but the characters themselves do not
11.9	Conceit	A kind of metaphor that compares two very different things in an unusual but clever way
11.10	Shakespearean sonnet	A poem of 14 lines written in iambic pentameter, ending with a rhyming couplet
11.11	Eponymous protagonist	A main character who the text is named after, e.g. Macbeth
11.12	Tragedy	A genre of play that features dramatic events, an unhappy ending and the downfall of the main character

Quiz 11: Key term definitions 1

TRACKER

Quiz	Date	Score
1		
2		
3		
4		
5		
6		

Got it? ☐

Quiz 11: Key term definitions 1

	Terms	Definitions
11.1	Iambic pentameter	
11.2	Blank verse	
11.3	Couplet	
11.4	Rhythm	
11.5	Metre	
11.6	Soliloquy	
11.7	Aside	
11.8	Dramatic irony	
11.9	Conceit	
11.10	Shakespearean sonnet	
11.11	Eponymous protagonist	
11.12	Tragedy	

Terms	Definitions
Couplet	
Soliloquy	
Conceit	
Tragedy	
Blank verse	
Rhythm	
Dramatic irony	
Shakespearean sonnet	
Iambic pentameter	
Metre	
Aside	
Eponymous protagonist	

Terms	Definitions
Shakespearean sonnet	
Iambic pentameter	
Metre	
Soliloquy	
Blank verse	
Conceit	
Aside	
Eponymous protagonist	
Dramatic irony	
Tragedy	
Couplet	
Rhythm	

Terms	Definitions
Soliloquy	
Tragedy	
Iambic pentameter	
Couplet	
Aside	
Metre	
Eponymous protagonist	
Dramatic irony	
Rhythm	
Shakespearean sonnet	
Blank verse	
Conceit	

Terms	Definitions
Couplet	
Soliloquy	
Conceit	
Tragedy	
Blank verse	
Rhythm	
Dramatic irony	
Shakespearean sonnet	
Iambic pentameter	
Metre	
Aside	
Eponymous protagonist	

Terms	Definitions
Shakespearean sonnet	
Iambic pentameter	
Metre	
Soliloquy	
Blank verse	
Conceit	
Aside	
Eponymous protagonist	
Dramatic irony	
Tragedy	
Couplet	
Rhythm	

Quiz 12: Key term spellings 1

Learn these spellings using the 'look, cover, write, check' method

		Look, cover	Write, check
12.1		iambic pentameter	*iambic pentameter*
12.2		blank verse	
12.3		couplet	
12.4		rhythm	
12.5		metre	
12.6		soliloquy	
12.7		aside	
12.8		dramatic irony	
12.9		conceit	
12.10		Shakespearean sonnet	
12.11		eponymous protagonist	
12.12		tragedy	

TRACKER

Quiz	Date	Score
1		
2		
3		
4		
5		
6		

Got it? ☐

	Look, cover	Write, check
12.1	iambic pentameter	
12.2	blank verse	
12.3	couplet	
12.4	rhythm	
12.5	metre	
12.6	soliloquy	
12.7	aside	
12.8	dramatic irony	
12.9	conceit	
12.10	Shakespearean sonnet	
12.11	eponymous protagonist	
12.12	tragedy	

Quiz 12: Key term spellings 1

Look, cover	Write, check
couplet	
soliloquy	
conceit	
tragedy	
blank verse	
rhythm	
dramatic irony	
Shakespearean sonnet	
iambic pentameter	
metre	
aside	
eponymous protagonist	

Look, cover	Write, check
Shakespearean sonnet	
iambic pentameter	
metre	
soliloquy	
blank verse	
conceit	
aside	
eponymous protagonist	
dramatic irony	
tragedy	
couplet	
rhythm	

Quiz 12: Key term spellings 1

Look, cover	Write, check
soliloquy	
tragedy	
iambic pentameter	
couplet	
aside	
metre	
eponymous protagonist	
dramatic irony	
rhythm	
Shakespearean sonnet	
blank verse	
conceit	

Look, cover	Write, check
couplet	
soliloquy	
conceit	
tragedy	
blank verse	
rhythm	
dramatic irony	
Shakespearean sonnet	
iambic pentameter	
metre	
aside	
eponymous protagonist	

Look, cover	Write, check
Shakespearean sonnet	
iambic pentameter	
metre	
soliloquy	
blank verse	
conceit	
aside	
eponymous protagonist	
dramatic irony	
tragedy	
couplet	
rhythm	

Quiz 13: Key term definitions 2

ANSWER KEY

	Terms	Definitions
13.1	Regicide	The murder of a king
13.2	Weird/wyrd	Fate, controlling human destiny
13.3	Hamartia	A fatal flaw that results in the downfall of a character
13.4	Hubris	Excessive arrogance or self-confidence
13.5	Catharsis	The idea that by watching tragedy, the audience can release their own extreme emotions
13.6	Anagnorisis	The moment in a text where a main character discovers the truth about herself/himself or someone else
13.7	Peripeteia	A sudden turning point or change in circumstances
13.8	Hallucination	Seeing or perceiving something that is not really there, e.g. when Macbeth sees the dagger
13.9	Existential crisis	A moment when a character questions whether their life has purpose or value
13.10	Chiasmus	Where words or ideas are repeated in reverse order, e.g. 'fair is foul and foul is fair'
13.11	Supernatural	Something that is beyond what is normal, or can't be explained by reason or science
13.12	Apparition	A ghost or ghostly image

TRACKER

Quiz	Date	Score
1		
2		
3		
4		
5		
6		

Got it? ☐

	Terms	Definitions
13.1	Regicide	
13.2	Weird/wyrd	
13.3	Hamartia	
13.4	Hubris	
13.5	Catharsis	
13.6	Anagnorisis	
13.7	Peripeteia	
13.8	Hallucination	
13.9	Existential crisis	
13.10	Chiasmus	
13.11	Supernatural	
13.12	Apparition	

Quiz 13: Key term definitions 2

Terms	Definitions
Hamartia	
Anagnorisis	
Existential crisis	
Apparition	
Weird/wyrd	
Hubris	
Hallucination	
Chiasmus	
Regicide	
Catharsis	
Peripeteia	
Supernatural	

Terms	Definitions
Chiasmus	
Regicide	
Catharsis	
Anagnorisis	
Weird/wyrd	
Existential crisis	
Peripeteia	
Supernatural	
Hallucination	
Apparition	
Hamartia	
Hubris	

Terms	Definitions
Anagnorisis	
Apparition	
Regicide	
Hamartia	
Peripeteia	
Catharsis	
Supernatural	
Hallucination	
Hubris	
Chiasmus	
Weird/wyrd	
Existential crisis	

Terms	Definitions
Hamartia	
Anagnorisis	
Existential crisis	
Apparition	
Weird/wyrd	
Hubris	
Hallucination	
Chiasmus	
Regicide	
Catharsis	
Peripeteia	
Supernatural	

Terms	Definitions
Chiasmus	
Regicide	
Catharsis	
Anagnorisis	
Weird/wyrd	
Existential crisis	
Peripeteia	
Supernatural	
Hallucination	
Apparition	
Hamartia	
Hubris	

Learn these spellings using the 'look, cover, write, check' method

	Look, cover	Write, check
14.1	regicide	*regicide*
14.2	weird/wyrd	
14.3	hamartia	
14.4	hubris	
14.5	catharsis	
14.6	anagnorisis	
14.7	peripeteia	
14.8	hallucination	
14.9	existential crisis	
14.10	chiasmus	
14.11	supernatural	
14.12	apparition	

TRACKER

Quiz	Date	Score
1		
2		
3		
4		
5		
6		

Got it? ☐

	Look, cover	Write, check
14.1	regicide	
14.2	weird/wyrd	
14.3	hamartia	
14.4	hubris	
14.5	catharsis	
14.6	anagnorisis	
14.7	peripeteia	
14.8	hallucination	
14.9	existential crisis	
14.10	chiasmus	
14.11	supernatural	
14.12	apparition	

Look, cover	Write, check
hamartia	
anagnorisis	
existential crisis	
apparition	
weird/wyrd	
hubris	
hallucination	
chiasmus	
regicide	
catharsis	
peripeteia	
supernatural	

Look, cover	Write, check
chiasmus	
regicide	
catharsis	
anagnorisis	
weird/wyrd	
existential crisis	
peripeteia	
supernatural	
hallucination	
apparition	
hamartia	
hubris	

Quiz 14: Key term spellings 2

Look, cover	Write, check
anagnorisis	
apparition	
regicide	
hamartia	
peripeteia	
catharsis	
supernatural	
hallucination	
hubris	
chiasmus	
weird/wyrd	
existential crisis	

Quiz 14: Key term spellings 2

Look, cover	Write, check
hamartia	
anagnorisis	
existential crisis	
apparition	
weird/wyrd	
hubris	
hallucination	
chiasmus	
regicide	
catharsis	
peripeteia	
supernatural	

Quiz 14: Key term spellings 2

Look, cover	Write, check
chiasmus	
regicide	
catharsis	
anagnorisis	
weird/wyrd	
existential crisis	
peripeteia	
supernatural	
hallucination	
apparition	
hamartia	
hubris	

Quotations

Knowing quotations alone is not enough to write great essays. You should do the following to prepare really well:

1. Memorise quotations using the 'look, cover, write, check' method. Alternatively, you could chant them out loud, or get friends to quiz you on them.

2. For each quotation, write down three or four ideas for analysis (e.g. powerful words, images, literary devices, context, structure).

3. Practise putting your quotations into your essays in timed conditions.

ANSWER KEY

15.1	'Fair is foul and foul is fair' (1.1)	Witches
15.2	'Stars, hide your fires/Let not light see my black and deep desires' (1.4)	Macbeth
15.3	'Come you spirits ... Unsex me here' (1.5)	Lady Macbeth
15.4	'Look like the innocent flower/But be the serpent under't' (1.5)	Lady Macbeth
15.5	'Is this a dagger which I see before me' (2.1)	Macbeth
15.6	'His silver skin laced with his golden blood' (2.3)	Macbeth
15.7	'There's daggers in men's smiles' (2.3)	Donalbain
15.8	'Upon my head they placed a fruitless crown' (3.1)	Macbeth
15.9	'Blood will have blood' (3.4)	Macbeth
15.10	'Something wicked this way comes' (4.1)	Witches
15.11	'Out, damned spot' (5.1)	Lady Macbeth
15.12	'...this dead butcher and his fiend-like queen' (5.8)	Malcolm

TRACKER

Quiz	Date	Score
1		
2		
3		
4		
5		
6		

Got it? ☐

15.1	'Fair is foul and foul is fair' (1.1)	
15.2	'Stars, hide your fires/Let not light see my black and deep desires' (1.4)	
15.3	'Come you spirits ... Unsex me here' (1.5)	
15.4	'Look like the innocent flower/But be the serpent under't' (1.5)	
15.5	'Is this a dagger which I see before me' (2.1)	
15.6	'His silver skin laced with his golden blood' (2.3)	
15.7	'There's daggers in men's smiles' (2.3)	
15.8	'Upon my head they placed a fruitless crown' (3.1)	
15.9	'Blood will have blood' (3.4)	
15.10	'Something wicked this way comes' (4.1)	
15.11	'Out, damned spot' (5.1)	
15.12	'...this dead butcher and his fiend-like queen' (5.8)	

'Come you spirits ... Unsex me here' (1.5)	
'His silver skin laced with his golden blood' (2.3)	
'Blood will have blood' (3.4)	
'...this dead butcher and his fiend-like queen' (5.8)	
'Stars, hide your fires/Let not light see my black and deep desires' (1.4)	
'Look like the innocent flower/But be the serpent under't' (1.5)	
'Upon my head they placed a fruitless crown' (3.1)	
'Something wicked this way comes' (4.1)	
'Fair is foul and foul is fair' (1.1)	
'Is this a dagger which I see before me' (2.1)	
'There's daggers in men's smiles' (2.3)	
'Out, damned spot' (5.1)	

'Something wicked this way comes' (4.1)	
'Fair is foul and foul is fair' (1.1)	
'Is this a dagger which I see before me' (2.1)	
'His silver skin laced with his golden blood' (2.3)	
'Stars, hide your fires/Let not light see my black and deep desires' (1.4)	
'Blood will have blood' (3.4)	
'There's daggers in men's smiles' (2.3)	
'Out, damned spot' (5.1)	
'Upon my head they placed a fruitless crown' (3.1)	
'...this dead butcher and his fiend-like queen' (5.8)	
'Come you spirits ... Unsex me here' (1.5)	
'Look like the innocent flower/But be the serpent under't' (1.5)	

'His silver skin laced with his golden blood' (2.3)	
'…this dead butcher and his fiend-like queen' (5.8)	
'Fair is foul and foul is fair' (1.1)	
'Come you spirits … Unsex me here' (1.5)	
'There's daggers in men's smiles' (2.3)	
'Is this a dagger which I see before me' (2.1)	
'Out, damned spot' (5.1)	
'Upon my head they placed a fruitless crown' (3.1)	
'Look like the innocent flower/But be the serpent under't' (1.5)	
'Something wicked this way comes' (4.1)	
'Stars, hide your fires/Let not light see my black and deep desires' (1.4)	
'Blood will have blood' (3.4)	

'Come you spirits ... Unsex me here' (1.5)	
'His silver skin laced with his golden blood' (2.3)	
'Blood will have blood' (3.4)	
'...this dead butcher and his fiend-like queen' (5.8)	
'Stars, hide your fires/Let not light see my black and deep desires' (1.4)	
'Look like the innocent flower/But be the serpent under't' (1.5)	
'Upon my head they placed a fruitless crown' (3.1)	
'Something wicked this way comes' (4.1)	
'Fair is foul and foul is fair' (1.1)	
'Is this a dagger which I see before me' (2.1)	
'There's daggers in men's smiles' (2.3)	
'Out, damned spot' (5.1)	

'Something wicked this way comes' (4.1)	
'Fair is foul and foul is fair' (1.1)	
'Is this a dagger which I see before me' (2.1)	
'His silver skin laced with his golden blood' (2.3)	
'Stars, hide your fires/Let not light see my black and deep desires' (1.4)	
'Blood will have blood' (3.4)	
'There's daggers in men's smiles' (2.3)	
'Out, damned spot' (5.1)	
'Upon my head they placed a fruitless crown' (3.1)	
'...this dead butcher and his fiend-like queen' (5.8)	
'Come you spirits ... Unsex me here' (1.5)	
'Look like the innocent flower/But be the serpent under't' (1.5)	

Quiz 16: Quotation bank 2

ANSWER KEY

16.1	'Unseamed him from the nave to the chops' (1.2)	Sergeant, about Macbeth
16.2	'All hail Macbeth that shall be king hereafter' (1.3)	Witches
16.3	'Lesser than Macbeth, and greater' (1.3)	Witches
16.4	'...too full o' the milk of human kindness' (1.5)	Lady Macbeth
16.5	'...screw your courage to the sticking place' (1.7)	Lady Macbeth
16.6	'My hands are of your colour but I shame/To wear a heart so white' (2.2)	Lady Macbeth
16.7	'...the fountain of your blood is stopp'd' (2.3)	Macbeth
16.8	'O horror, horror, horror! Tongue nor heart/Cannot conceive nor name thee!' (2.3)	Macduff
16.9	'Full of scorpions is my mind' (3.2)	Macbeth
16.10	'Hence, horrible shadow! Unreal mockery, hence!' (3.4)	Macbeth
16.11	'He has no children. All my pretty ones?' (4.3)	Macduff
16.12	'Life's but a walking shadow, a poor player' (5.5)	Macbeth

TRACKER

Quiz	Date	Score
1		
2		
3		
4		
5		
6		

Got it? ☐

16.1	'Unseamed him from the nave to the chops' (1.2)	
16.2	'All hail Macbeth that shall be king hereafter' (1.3)	
16.3	'Lesser than Macbeth, and greater' (1.3)	
16.4	'...too full o' the milk of human kindness' (1.5)	
16.5	'...screw your courage to the sticking place' (1.7)	
16.6	'My hands are of your colour but I shame/To wear a heart so white' (2.2)	
16.7	'...the fountain of your blood is stopp'd' (2.3)	
16.8	'O horror, horror, horror! Tongue nor heart/Cannot conceive nor name thee!' (2.3)	
16.9	'Full of scorpions is my mind' (3.2)	
16.10	'Hence, horrible shadow! Unreal mockery, hence!' (3.4)	
16.11	'He has no children. All my pretty ones?' (4.3)	
16.12	'Life's but a walking shadow, a poor player' (5.5)	

'Lesser than Macbeth, and greater' (1.3)	
'My hands are of your colour but I shame/To wear a heart so white' (2.2)	
'Full of scorpions is my mind' (3.2)	
'Life's but a walking shadow, a poor player' (5.5)	
'All hail Macbeth that shall be king hereafter' (1.3)	
'...too full o' the milk of human kindness' (1.5)	
'O horror, horror, horror! Tongue nor heart/Cannot conceive nor name thee!' (2.3)	
'Hence, horrible shadow! Unreal mockery, hence!' (3.4)	
'Unseamed him from the nave to the chops' (1.2)	
'...screw your courage to the sticking place' (1.7)	
'...the fountain of your blood is stopp'd' (2.3)	
'He has no children. All my pretty ones?' (4.3)	

'Hence, horrible shadow! Unreal mockery, hence!' (3.4)	
'Unseamed him from the nave to the chops' (1.2)	
'...screw your courage to the sticking place' (1.7)	
'My hands are of your colour but I shame/To wear a heart so white' (2.2)	
'All hail Macbeth that shall be king hereafter' (1.3)	
'Full of scorpions is my mind' (3.2)	
'...the fountain of your blood is stopp'd' (2.3)	
'He has no children. All my pretty ones?' (4.3)	
'O horror, horror, horror! Tongue nor heart/Cannot conceive nor name thee!' (2.3)	
'Life's but a walking shadow, a poor player' (5.5)	
'Lesser than Macbeth, and greater' (1.3)	
'...too full o' the milk of human kindness' (1.5)	

'My hands are of your colour but I shame/To wear a heart so white' (2.2)	
'Life's but a walking shadow, a poor player' (5.5)	
'Unseamed him from the nave to the chops' (1.2)	
'Lesser than Macbeth, and greater' (1.3)	
'...the fountain of your blood is stopp'd' (2.3)	
'...screw your courage to the sticking place' (1.7)	
'He has no children. All my pretty ones?' (4.3)	
'O horror, horror, horror! Tongue nor heart/Cannot conceive nor name thee!' (2.3)	
'...too full o' the milk of human kindness' (1.5)	
'Hence, horrible shadow! Unreal mockery, hence!' (3.4)	
'All hail Macbeth that shall be king hereafter' (1.3)	
'Full of scorpions is my mind' (3.2)	

'Lesser than Macbeth, and greater' (1.3)	
'My hands are of your colour but I shame/To wear a heart so white' (2.2)	
'Full of scorpions is my mind' (3.2)	
'Life's but a walking shadow, a poor player' (5.5)	
'All hail Macbeth that shall be king hereafter' (1.3)	
'…too full o' the milk of human kindness' (1.5)	
'O horror, horror, horror! Tongue nor heart/Cannot conceive nor name thee!' (2.3)	
'Hence, horrible shadow! Unreal mockery, hence!' (3.4)	
'Unseamed him from the nave to the chops' (1.2)	
'…screw your courage to the sticking place' (1.7)	
'…the fountain of your blood is stopp'd' (2.3)	
'He has no children. All my pretty ones?' (4.3)	

'Hence, horrible shadow! Unreal mockery, hence!' (3.4)	
'Unseamed him from the nave to the chops' (1.2)	
'...screw your courage to the sticking place' (1.7)	
'My hands are of your colour but I shame/To wear a heart so white' (2.2)	
'All hail Macbeth that shall be king hereafter' (1.3)	
'Full of scorpions is my mind' (3.2)	
'...the fountain of your blood is stopp'd' (2.3)	
'He has no children. All my pretty ones?' (4.3)	
'O horror, horror, horror! Tongue nor heart/Cannot conceive nor name thee!' (2.3)	
'Life's but a walking shadow, a poor player' (5.5)	
'Lesser than Macbeth, and greater' (1.3)	
'...too full o' the milk of human kindness' (1.5)	

ANSWER KEY

17.1	'...chance may crown me, without my stir' (1.3)	Macbeth
17.2	'So wither'd and so wild in their attire/That look not like the inhabitants o' the earth' (1.3)	Banquo
17.3	'Why do you dress me in borrowed robes?' (1.3)	Macbeth
17.4	'Make thick my blood' (1.5)	Lady Macbeth
17.5	'I have given suck, and know/How tender 'tis to love the babe that milks me' (1.7)	Lady Macbeth
17.6	'Macbeth does murder sleep' (2.2)	Macbeth
17.7	'Knock, knock, knock! Who's there, i' th' name of Beelzebub?' (2.3)	Porter
17.8	'And his gash'd stabs looked like a breach in nature' (3.1)	Macbeth
17.9	'Double, double, toil and trouble' (4.1)	Witches
17.10	'All the perfumes of Arabia will not sweeten this little hand' (5.1)	Lady Macbeth
17.11	'The Thane of Fife had a wife. Where is she now?' (5.1)	Lady Macbeth
17.12	'I bear a charmed life' (5.8)	Macbeth

TRACKER

Quiz	Date	Score
1		
2		
3		
4		
5		
6		

Got it? ☐

17.1	'...chance may crown me, without my stir' (1.3)	
17.2	'So wither'd and so wild in their attire/That look not like the inhabitants o' the earth' (1.3)	
17.3	'Why do you dress me in borrowed robes?' (1.3)	
17.4	'Make thick my blood' (1.5)	
17.5	'I have given suck, and know/How tender 'tis to love the babe that milks me' (1.7)	
17.6	'Macbeth does murder sleep' (2.2)	
17.7	'Knock, knock, knock! Who's there, i' th' name of Beelzebub?' (2.3)	
17.8	'And his gash'd stabs looked like a breach in nature' (3.1)	
17.9	'Double, double, toil and trouble' (4.1)	
17.10	'All the perfumes of Arabia will not sweeten this little hand' (5.1)	
17.11	'The Thane of Fife had a wife. Where is she now?' (5.1)	
17.12	'I bear a charmed life' (5.8)	

'Why do you dress me in borrowed robes?' (1.3)	
'Macbeth does murder sleep' (2.2)	
'Double, double, toil and trouble' (4.1)	
'I bear a charmed life' (5.8)	
'So wither'd and so wild in their attire/That look not like the inhabitants o' the earth' (1.3)	
'Make thick my blood' (1.5)	
'And his gash'd stabs looked like a breach in nature' (3.1)	
'All the perfumes of Arabia will not sweeten this little hand' (5.1)	
'...chance may crown me, without my stir' (1.3)	
'I have given suck, and know/How tender 'tis to love the babe that milks me' (1.7)	
'Knock, knock, knock! Who's there, i' th' name of Beelzebub?' (2.3)	
'The Thane of Fife had a wife. Where is she now?' (5.1)	

'All the perfumes of Arabia will not sweeten this little hand' (5.1)	
'...chance may crown me, without my stir' (1.3)	
'I have given suck, and know/How tender 'tis to love the babe that milks me' (1.7)	
'Macbeth does murder sleep' (2.2)	
'So wither'd and so wild in their attire/That look not like the inhabitants o' the earth' (1.3)	
'Double, double, toil and trouble' (4.1)	
'Knock, knock, knock! Who's there, i' th' name of Beelzebub?' (2.3)	
'The Thane of Fife had a wife. Where is she now?' (5.1)	
'And his gash'd stabs looked like a breach in nature' (3.1)	
'I bear a charmed life' (5.8)	
'Why do you dress me in borrowed robes?' (1.3)	
'Make thick my blood' (1.5)	

'Macbeth does murder sleep' (2.2)	
'I bear a charmed life' (5.8)	
'...chance may crown me, without my stir' (1.3)	
'Why do you dress me in borrowed robes?' (1.3)	
'Knock, knock, knock! Who's there, i' th' name of Beelzebub?' (2.3)	
'I have given suck, and know/How tender 'tis to love the babe that milks me' (1.7)	
'The Thane of Fife had a wife. Where is she now?' (5.1)	
'And his gash'd stabs looked like a breach in nature' (3.1)	
'Make thick my blood' (1.5)	
'All the perfumes of Arabia will not sweeten this little hand' (5.1)	
'So wither'd and so wild in their attire/That look not like the inhabitants o' the earth' (1.3)	
'Double, double, toil and trouble' (4.1)	

'Why do you dress me in borrowed robes?' (1.3)	
'Macbeth does murder sleep' (2.2)	
'Double, double, toil and trouble' (4.1)	
'I bear a charmed life' (5.8)	
'So wither'd and so wild in their attire/That look not like the inhabitants o' the earth' (1.3)	
'Make thick my blood' (1.5)	
'And his gash'd stabs looked like a breach in nature' (3.1)	
'All the perfumes of Arabia will not sweeten this little hand' (5.1)	
'...chance may crown me, without my stir' (1.3)	
'I have given suck, and know/How tender 'tis to love the babe that milks me' (1.7)	
'Knock, knock, knock! Who's there, i' th' name of Beelzebub?' (2.3)	
'The Thane of Fife had a wife. Where is she now?' (5.1)	

'All the perfumes of Arabia will not sweeten this little hand' (5.1)	
'...chance may crown me, without my stir' (1.3)	
'I have given suck, and know/How tender 'tis to love the babe that milks me' (1.7)	
'Macbeth does murder sleep' (2.2)	
'So wither'd and so wild in their attire/That look not like the inhabitants o' the earth' (1.3)	
'Double, double, toil and trouble' (4.1)	
'Knock, knock, knock! Who's there, i' th' name of Beelzebub?' (2.3)	
'The Thane of Fife had a wife. Where is she now?' (5.1)	
'And his gash'd stabs looked like a breach in nature' (3.1)	
'I bear a charmed life' (5.8)	
'Why do you dress me in borrowed robes?' (1.3)	
'Make thick my blood' (1.5)	